DISCOVERING THE UNITED STATES

California

BY JEAN KUO LEE

Kids Core
An Imprint of Abdo Publishing
abdobooks.com

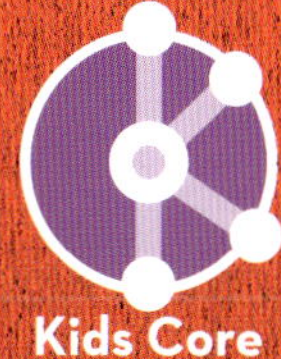

abdobooks.com

Published by Abdo Publishing, a division of ABDO, PO Box 398166, Minneapolis, Minnesota 55439.

Printed in China.
052024
092024

Cover Photo: Lynn Yeh/Shutterstock Images
Interior Photos: Science History Images/Alamy, 4–5; iStockphoto, 7 (top left), 13, 26, 28 (top right); Shishka Bob/Shutterstock Images, 7 (top right); Oksana Akhtanina/iStockphoto, 7 (bottom left); Shutterstock Images, 7 (bottom right), 20–21, 22, 24; Chizhevskaya Ekaterina/Shutterstock Images, 8, 28 (bottom); Mark Ralston/AFP/Getty Images, 10–11; Gado/Archive Photos/Getty Images, 12; Dania Maxwell/Los Angeles Times/Getty Images, 14; Jamie Squire/Getty Images Sport/Getty Images, 15; Uladzik Kryhin/Shutterstock Images, 17; Lowe Llaguno/Shutterstock Images, 18; Red Line Editorial, 28 (top left), 29

Editor: Christa Kelly
Series Designer: Katharine Hale

Library of Congress Control Number: 2023949340

Publisher's Cataloging-in-Publication Data

Names: Lee, Jean Kuo, author.
Title: California / by Jean Kuo Lee
Description: Minneapolis, Minnesota: Abdo Publishing, 2025 | Series: Discovering the United States | Includes online resources and index.
Identifiers: ISBN 9781098293758 (lib. bdg.) | ISBN 9798384913023 (ebook)
Subjects: LCSH: U.S. states--Juvenile literature. | California--History--Juvenile literature. | Western States (U.S.)--Juvenile literature. | Physical geography--United States--Juvenile literature.
Classification: DDC 973--dc23

All population data taken from:
"Estimates of Population by Sex, Race, and Hispanic Origin: April 1, 2020 to July 1, 2022." *US Census Bureau, Population Division*, June 2023, census.gov.

CONTENTS

CHAPTER 1
Gold Rush 4

CHAPTER 2
The People of California 10

CHAPTER 3
Places in California 20

State Map 28
Glossary 30
Online Resources 31
Learn More 31
Index 32
About the Author 32

About 300,000 people flocked to California after James Wilson Marshall discovered gold in 1848.

Gold Rush

It was a chilly January morning in 1848. James Wilson Marshall began his daily work building a sawmill in Coloma, California. He was inspecting a ditch that workers had dug when he spotted something glistening in the cool water below.

The water was filled with small, shiny flecks. Marshall picked one up. He had found gold.

Marshall tried to keep his discovery a secret. But the news got out quickly. People from around the world raced to California. They were hoping to get rich by finding gold themselves. The California Gold Rush had begun.

Forty-Niners

The people who came to California in search of gold first arrived in 1849. This earned them the nickname forty-niners. Many came from the East Coast of the United States. Others came from Mexico. Some even came from China and France.

California Facts

DATE OF STATEHOOD
September 9, 1850

CAPITAL
Sacramento

POPULATION
39,029,342

AREA
163,695 square miles
(423,968 sq km)

STATE BIRD

California quail

STATE TREE

California redwood

STATE FLOWER

California poppy

STATE MAMMAL

Grizzly bear

Each US state has a different population, size, and capital city. States also have state symbols.

California's Land

California is in the US region called the West.

The state is bordered by Oregon to the north.

Mount Whitney is part of the Sierra Nevada. It is the tallest mountain in the continental United States.

Nevada and Arizona border California to the east. Mexico is to the south. California's western border is the Pacific Ocean.

California has sandy beaches and cliffs on its coast. It has giant redwood forests in the northwest. The forests are home to black bears. The Sierra Nevada Mountain range covers a large part of central California. Mountain lions live in the Sierra Nevada. East of the mountains are deserts.

Summers along California's coast are warm and dry. The weather is hotter **inland**. California winters are cool and rainy. The mountains are the only areas in the state with heavy snowfall.

Explore Online

Visit the website below. Does it give any new information about California's geography that wasn't in Chapter One?

California

abdocorelibrary.com/discovering-california

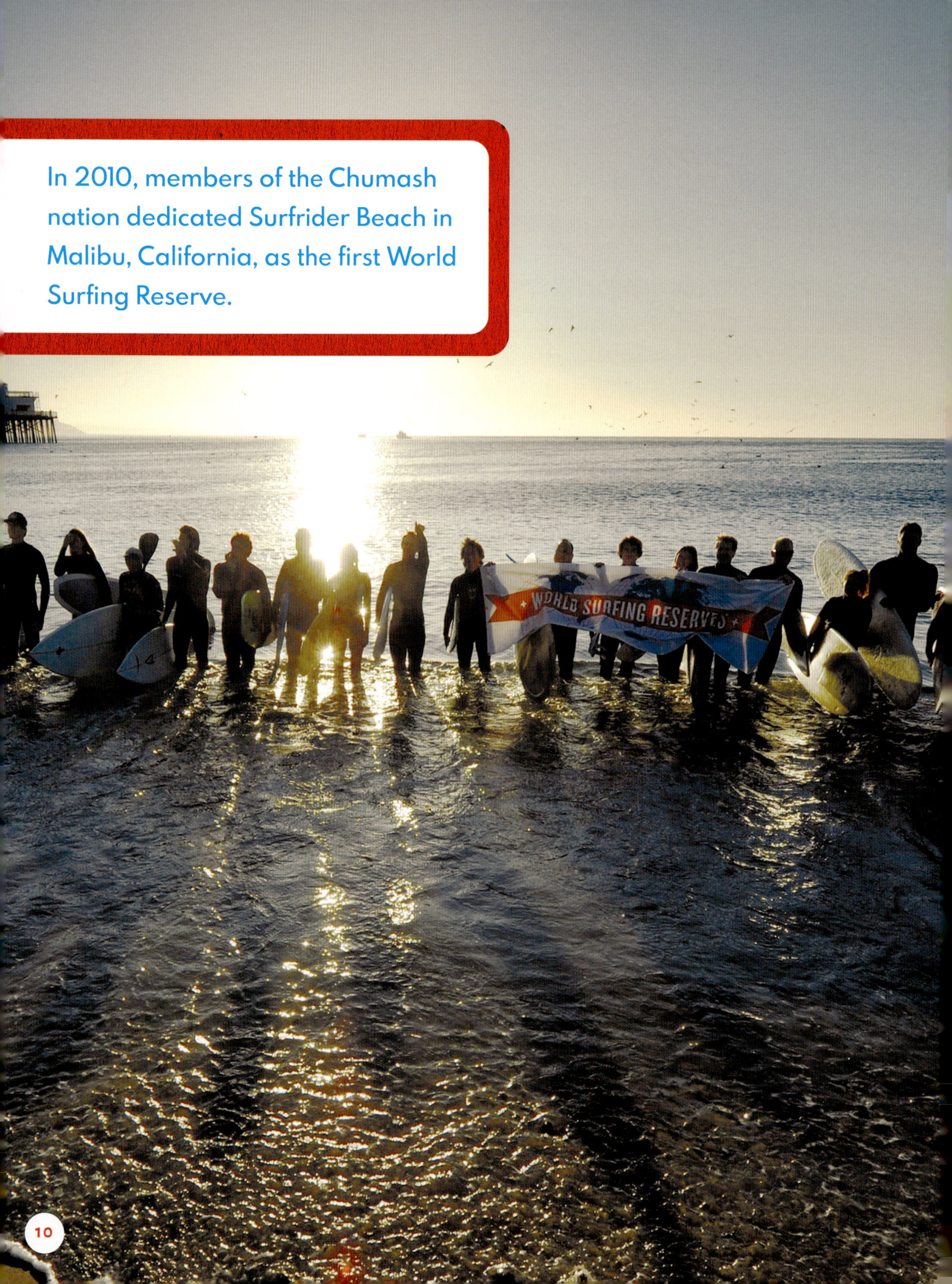

In 2010, members of the Chumash nation dedicated Surfrider Beach in Malibu, California, as the first World Surfing Reserve.

The People of California

American Indians began living in California at least 12,000 years ago. Over time, they formed more than 100 nations. These included the Chumash, Maidu, and Mojave nations. In the 1700s, Europeans arrived. They **colonized** the land.

California miners used long chutes called sluices to sift gold from the water.

Many American Indians were forced to leave the region.

In 1848, gold was discovered in California. More than 300,000 people rushed to the state in hopes of getting rich. Big cities like San Francisco were created to support the miners. Two years later, California became the thirty-first state in the nation.

The “Bear Flag” was adopted as California’s official flag in 1911.

Today, more than 40 percent of people in California are Hispanic or Latino. About 35 percent of Californians are white. More than 16 percent are Asian. About 6.5 percent are Black. Almost 2 percent of people in California are American Indian.

There are roughly 85,000 Latino-owned businesses in California.

California Culture

About one out of every three adults in California are **immigrants**. Almost half of the children in California have at least one parent who was born in another country. This means that California is very **diverse**. The food found in the state comes from all over the world.

Venus, *left*, and Serena Williams are considered two of the greatest tennis players in history.

Mexican tacos, Japanese sushi, and an Italian stew called cioppino are all popular dishes.

Many record-setting athletes grew up in the state. Tennis players Venus and Serena Williams grew up in Compton. Golfer Tiger Woods and soccer star Alex Morgan are also Californians.

Football star Tom Brady and baseball legend Barry Bonds are both from San Mateo.

Industries

California is well-known for its entertainment industry. Many movies and television shows are made in California. The state is also the center of the nation's computer and internet industry. Google and Apple are two major technology

Silicon Valley

Silicon Valley is a region in California near San Jose. Silicon is a common material in electronics. The area is called Silicon Valley because many computer and internet companies are there. Google and Apple are headquartered in Silicon Valley.

Google's offices in Mountain View, California, are called the Googleplex.

companies in California. Google's search engine handles more than 70 percent of the world's online search requests. Apple makes computers and smartphones.

Many people in California work on farms. Farmers in the state grow a variety of crops.

In 2022, California's most produced crops included lettuce, almonds, and strawberries.

California farmers grow most of the United States' fruits and nuts. Other Californians work in the service industry. These people work in stores and restaurants. They also take care of the 200 million tourists who visit California every year. With its big population and many companies, California has the largest **economy** of any US state.

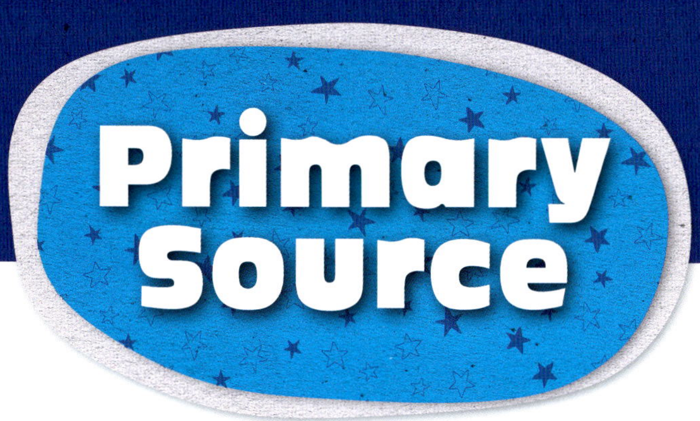

Walter Colton was a newspaper editor. He wrote about the California Gold Rush:

> The excitement produced was intense. . . . The blacksmith dropped his hammer, . . . the baker his loaf. . . . All were off for the mines, some on horses, some on carts, and some on crutches.

Source: Walter Colton. *Three Years in California.* A. S. Barnes & Co., A. S. Barnes & Co., H. W. Derby & Co., 1850. *Library of Congress,* loc.gov. Accessed 8 Dec. 2023

What's the Big Idea?

Read the primary source carefully. What is its main idea? Explain how the main idea is supported by details.

The California state capitol building took 14 years to build. It was finished in 1874.

Places in California

The capital of California is Sacramento. It is located in the north-central part of the state. Sacramento is one of the most **populated** cities in California.

Los Angeles is the most populated city in California.

A replica of Hogwarts Castle is one of the many attractions at Universal Studios Hollywood.

It is also the second most populated city in the United States. Los Angeles is located in southern California. The Hollywood Sign, which looks over Los Angeles, is a symbol of the city's movie and television industry. The Hollywood neighborhood is home to many film studios. It is also home to Universal Studios Hollywood. This amusement park has film-themed rides and attractions. Millions of people visit the park each year.

San Diego is the oldest city in California. It was founded as a Spanish settlement in 1769. San Diego sits near California's border with Mexico.

Parks

California has nine national parks. That is the most of any state. Yosemite National Park is California's most popular park. Visitors from all over the world come to see the park's granite cliffs and beautiful waterfalls.

Joshua Tree National Park is slightly larger than the state of Rhode Island. It is located in the desert east of Los Angeles. People come to explore its huge boulders and unique Joshua trees.

The hottest temperature in US history was recorded in Death Valley. It reached 134 degrees Fahrenheit (57°C) on July 10, 1913.

Death Valley National Park is the state's largest national park. It covers 5,270 square miles (13,650 sq km). The park is made up of sand dunes and sandstone **canyons**. It is home to Badwater Basin. The basin is the lowest point in North America.

Disneyland is a theme park in Anaheim. It was created by filmmaker Walt Disney in 1955.

State Parks

In addition to its national parks, California has 280 state parks. The parks cover more than 1.6 million acres (700,000 ha) of land. More than 68 million people visit California state parks every year.

Construction for the Golden Gate Bridge began in 1933. The bridge was completed in 1937.

Today, it is one of the most popular tourist destinations in the country. Visitors can ride roller coasters and meet characters from popular Disney movies. The park also has its own restaurants and hotels.

The Golden Gate Bridge is another popular landmark in California. It is located in San Francisco in northern California. The bridge is 1.7 miles (2.7 km) long. It is also 746 feet (227 m) high. The bridge allows people to cross San Francisco Bay. More than 100,000 cars cross the bridge every day.

California is an exciting place to explore. It has a rich history. Whether people are sports fans, movie buffs, or lovers of the outdoors, the state has something for everyone.

Further Evidence

Look at the website below. Does it give any new evidence to support Chapter Three?

Yosemite National Park California

abdocorelibrary.com/discovering-california

State Map

KEY

Capital

Park

City or town

Point of interest

Golden Gate Bridge

Mount Whitney

California: The Golden State

Glossary

canyons
deep, narrow valleys cut by rivers through rock. This process, called erosion, can take thousands or millions of years

colonized
moved into and took control of an area

diverse
having many different kinds of people

economy
the system of how money is made and used within a particular country or region

immigrants
people who move to a different country

inland
of or relating to land that is further away from an ocean

populated
settled or lived in

Online Resources

To learn more about California, visit our free resource websites below.

Visit **abdocorelibrary.com** or scan this QR code for free Common Core resources for teachers and students, including vetted activities, multimedia, and booklinks, for deeper subject comprehension.

Visit **abdobooklinks.com** or scan this QR code for free additional online weblinks for further learning. These links are routinely monitored and updated to provide the most current information available.

Learn More

Katz, Susan B. *The Story of Walt Disney.* Rockridge Press, 2022.

Payne, Stefanie. *The National Parks.* DK, 2020.

Tieck, Sarah. *California.* Abdo, 2020.

Index

Apple, 16–17

Chumash nation, 11
Colton, Walter, 19

Disneyland, 25–26

food, 14–15, 18

gold, 6, 12, 19
Golden Gate Bridge, 26–27
Google, 16–17

Los Angeles, 21–23

Maidu nation, 11
Marshall, James Wilson, 5–6
Mojave nation, 11

national parks, 23, 25, 27

Sacramento, 21
San Diego, 23
San Francisco, 12, 26–27
Sierra Nevada, 9
sports, 15–16, 27
state symbols, 7

Universal Studios, 22

About the Author

Jean Kuo Lee is a writer who has lived in California for more than 30 years. Her favorite place in California is Tenaya Lake in Yosemite National Park.